D0402866

Published by Barbour Publishing, Inc., P.O. Box 719, Uhrichsville, Ohio 44683
http://www.barbourbooks.com

Member of the
Evangelical Christian
Publishers Association

Printed in China.

TWO
are better than one

ELLYN SANNA

BARBOUR
PUBLISHING, INC.

Two are better than one,
because they have a good
reward for their toil.
For if they fall,
one will lift up the other.

ECCLESIASTES 4:9–10 NRSV

I love you because. . .

- joys are greater when we're together;
- the road is smoother when we journey side by side;
- you bring out the best in me;
- I trust your commitment and respect for me;
- you help me to know God;
- and in the end, I love you just because you're you
       . . .and I always will!

One

*Joys are greater
when we're together. . .*

Two are better than one,
*   because when we're together. . .*

- I laugh more.
- even rainy days seem bright.
- food tastes better.
- music sounds better.
- I enjoy my family and friends even more.
- I feel God's joy everywhere I turn.

All who joy would win
Must share it,
Happiness was born a twin.

LORD BYRON

I know you've heard all the jokes about love and commitment. . .words like "ball and chain" and references to the end of freedom. But for me, falling in love with you has been just the opposite sort of experience. I don't feel weighted down and restricted; I feel as though I now have wings to fly. Our love has not ended my freedom; instead I feel as though love has flung open doors I never even guessed existed—and I am free to walk into brand-new worlds of growth and wonder. Loving you is a joyful adventure that just keeps getting better.

Anything, everything, little or big becomes
an adventure when the right person shares it.

KATHLEEN NORRIS

. . .

*No joys are above
The pleasures of love.*

JOHN DRYDEN

. . .

Paradise is always where love dwells.

JEAN PAUL RICHTER

Two

*The road is smoother
when we journey side by side...*

*Two are better than one,
         because when we're together. . .*

- I have courage to face the challenges life brings.
- I always know I have someone on my side.
- you inspire me to keep going when I feel like giving up.
- you comfort me when I'm feeling sad.
- you believe in me even when no one else does.
- I know I can always count on you to care and understand.

How blessed I am that
I can walk beside you,
lean upon you,
and live within the warmth of your love.

ROY LESSIN

*Good company on a journey
makes the way seem shorter.*

IZAAK WALTON

. . .

A knowledge that another has felt as we have felt,
and seen things not much otherwise
than we have seen them,
will continue to the end to
be one of life's choicest blessings.

ROBERT LOUIS STEVENSON

$\mathcal{I}$ am so glad we can travel life's road together. I know that if I stumble, you will always be there to catch me and help me get on my feet again. Together, even the hardest, darkest journeys seem brighter and not so long.

If you should move ahead of me on our journey, I promise to hurry to catch up. And if you ever lag behind, I will wait for you. I would never want to lose the companionship we share.

Three

*You bring out
the best in me. . .*

Two are better than one,
*   because when we're together. . .*

- I feel attractive even when the mirror says I'm not.
- I like myself better.
- I feel stronger.
- I have more courage to face life's trials.
- My heart is filled with love for others.
- I strive to be all that God has called me to be.

Your best friend is
the person who brings out of you
the best that is within you.

HENRY FORD

Trust each other again and again.
When the trust level gets high enough,
people transcend apparent limitations and
discover new and awesome abilities. . . .

DAVID ARMISTEAD

. . .

Snowflakes are a fragile thing individually,
but look at what they can do
when they stick together.

FERNANDO BONAVENTURA

. . .

Draw strength from each other.

JAMES A. RENIER

Two are Better than One

In a perfect union the man and the woman are like a
strung bow. Who is to say whether the string bends
the bow, or the bow tightens the strings? Yet male bow
and female string are in harmony with each other, and
their arrow can be aimed. Unstrung the bow hangs
aimless; the cord flaps idly.

CYRIL CONNOLLY

. . .

We each have a spark of life inside us,
and we must set off that spark in one another.

KENNY AUSUBEL

. . .

Love betters what is best.

WILLIAM WORDSWORTH

*A*s close as you and I are, I know you can't help but see my many weaknesses—all my faults and ugly warts, the small, silly sins I hide from everyone else, as well as those bigger, darker flaws I'd rather not face. And yet you still love me; you look past all the less beautiful things about me, and you affirm in me all that is good and true and beautiful.

And somehow, because I know you love me, I find myself becoming a better person. Supported by your love, I have the courage to face my sins and offer them to God; inspired by your love, I find myself growing to new levels of freedom and maturity; and in the warm light of your love, I look into the mirror, and I like the person I see.

Four

*I trust your commitment
and respect for me. . .*

*Two are better than one,
    because I always know. . .*

• I can depend on you to be true to me.
• you and I walk with God as equals.
• time won't change your commitment to our love.
• you respect my right to be me.
• I can rest on the foundation of our love.
• our love will never fail.

Perfect love

cannot be without equality.

ANONYMOUS

All true love is grounded on esteem.

GEORGE BUCKINGHAM

. . .

Equality is the firmest bond of love.

GOTTHOLD EPHRAIM LESSING

. . .

It is as absurd today that a man can't love
one woman all the time as it is to say that
a violinist needs several violins to play
the same piece of music.

HONORÉ DE BALZAC

[Love] bears all things, believes all things, hopes all things, endures all things. Love never ends.

1 CORINTHIANS 13:7–8 NRSV

. . .

We find rest in those we love,
and we provide a resting place in ourselves
for those who love us.

BERNARD OF CLAIRVAUX

. . .

Let me not to the marriage of true minds
Admit impediments. Love is not love
Which alters when it alteration finds.

WILLIAM SHAKESPEARE

Some days it seems as though all we can do is fight. Every time we open our mouths, we're snapping and snipping at each other. I get on your nerves; you drive me crazy; and there just doesn't seem to be any way we can live in peace.

And yet even then, I know I can count on your commitment to our love; no matter how much we fight, the promises we've made won't evaporate or disappear. I rely on your respect; I trust you to never uproot the foundation of our life together. I hope you know you can trust me in the same way.

Sometimes our fights clear the air, and we end up closer than we were before. In the end, though, the best thing about fighting is the part that comes next—making up!

Five

*You help me
to know God...*

*Two are better than one,
        because your love. . .*

- inspires me to grow in faith.
- gives me courage to climb the spiritual mountains in my life.
- teaches me to follow God's way.
- helps me understand God's love.
- gives me a glimpse of Jesus.
- reminds me that grace is never based on any effort of my own.

God in His ample love embraces our love with. . .
a sort of tenderness,
and we must tread the way to Him hand in hand.

SHELDON VANAUKEN

. . .

We are the gift of
the living God to one another.

REINE DUELL BETHANY

. . .

True love is that which ennobles the personality,
fortifies the heart, and sanctifies the existence.

HENRI FRÉDÉRIC AMIEL

 never did anything to deserve your love— and yet you give me your love with open arms. Through you I see a new picture of Jesus, the One who loved me, even when I didn't deserve His love, the One who daily comes to me with His arms held out, offering me Himself. The earthly love we share shows me a picture of the heavenly love I can hardly dare to grasp. God shows me His heart through you.

Six

I love you just because
you're you. . .
and I always will!

Two are better than one,
because. . .

- when I'm bored, you make me smile.
- when I'm sad, you cheer me up.
- you make my life interesting just by being you.
- I can't imagine living without you.
- there's no one with whom I'd rather spend my life.
- as time goes by, I learn to love you more.

The best thing to hold onto in life
is each other.

AUDREY HEPBURN

*Love in the heart is better than
honey in the mouth.*

ANONYMOUS

. . .

Did I choose you?
Did you choose me?
And what difference does it make?
All that really matters. . .
Is that we chose
Together.

LOIS WYSE

Remember when we first met? We could have smiled and walked away; we could have chosen to follow after other relationships. Aren't you glad we chose to get to know each other better? And then time after time, we chose to go deeper in our relationship. Again and again, we chose to promise each other still more of our hearts.

I'm so glad we did. You are the person I love best in all the world.

And I choose to love you more and more as time goes by.

Young love is a flame; very pretty,
often very hot and fierce,
but still only light and flickering.
The love of the older and disciplined heart is as coals,
deep-burning, unquenchable.

HENRY WARD BEECHER

. . .

Love is a true renewer.

ROGER DEBUSSY-RABUTIN

. . .

Those who have loved longest love best.

SAMUEL JOHNSON

I love thee, I love thee,
'Tis all that I can say.
It is my vision in the night,
My dreaming in the day.

THOMAS HOOD

. . .

Love has no age, as it is always renewing.

BLAISE PASCAL

. . .

The lover's soul dwells in the body of another.

LATIN PROVERB

From the beginning and to the end of time,
Love reads without letters and
counts without arithmetic.

JOHN RUSKIN

. . .

Mutual love, the crown of all our bliss.

JOHN MILTON

. . .

In the end,
I can never express all that you mean to me.
I hope you understand how much I love you.
I'm so glad that God made you—
and I'm so grateful that I share my life with you.

Don't ask me to leave you!
Let me go with you.
Wherever you go, I will go;
wherever you live; I will live.
Your people will be my people,
and your God will be my God.
Wherever you die, I will die,
and that is where I will be buried.
May the Lord's worst punishment come upon me
if I let anything but death separate me from you.

RUTH 1:16–17 TEV

. . .

Thank You, Lord, that we can journey through
our life together.
Thank You for giving us each other.
Help us to choose each other over and over
for the rest of our lives.
Amen.